LIFE AFTER THE
DINOSAURS

Written by Mary O'Neill
Illustrated & Designed by John Bindon

Published in 1989 by
The Hamlyn Publishing Group Limited
Michelin House, 81 Fulham Road, London SW3 6RB
© Copyright 1989 Mokum Publishing Inc.
Published in association with Vanwell Publishing Limited
U.K. edition edited by Neil Curtis Publishing Services
ISBN 0 600 56616 1
Printed in Canada

HAMLYN

About this Book

Millions of years before our time, a fascinating group of animals called dinosaurs roamed the earth. In their time, there were hundreds of different types of dinosaurs. Among them were the largest creatures that have ever walked on land. Not all were so huge, however. Others were as small as a chicken and could run at 24 kilometres an hour (15 mph).

Then something disastrous happened to the dinosaurs about sixty-five million years ago. They disappeared off the face of the earth, together with most other large creatures. What happened to them is one of our greatest mysteries. Scientists will puzzle for many years over why so many of these ancient creatures died out at the same time.

Of course, not all types of animals were wiped out then. Many survived the disaster that killed the dinosaurs. And with their greatest competitors gone, these survivors had the world to themselves. Over the millions years since then, they have developed into many groups o animals. Some are as amazing as the dinosaurs themselves.

In this book, we'll look at some of the animals that have come and gone in the natural world since the death of the dinosaurs. You might recogniz some of these creatures. But others were like nothing on earth today. Read on and find out more about life after the dinosaurs.

Table of Contents

History of the Earth

Just how old is the earth? Its history stretches back further than our imaginations. The oldest living people today are just over 100 years old. The earth is about forty-five million times older than they are!

Scientists think life on earth started about 4500 million years ago when the first single-celled creatures appeared. These tiny bacteria and algae began a chain of life that has led to more and more complex creatures and plants ever since. The dinosaurs were just one of many kinds of life that developed over these billions of years.

The Living Oceans

If you wanted to live among earth's oldest creatures, you'd have to be a good swimmer. Life first developed in the oceans. The earliest animals were soft sea creatures like today's jellyfish and worms. These appeared about 700 million years ago during a time called the Precambrian (Pree-CAM-bree-un). Most animals and plants from that time probably had soft bodies. They didn't have the bones, shells and stems that can easily fossilize.

Animal life remained in the waters through the next 300 million years of history. Shelled creatures appeared in the oceans during a time called the Cambrian (CAM-bree-un)—about 570 million years ago. The Cambrian was the earliest part of the Palaeozoic (Pay-lee-oh-ZO-ik) Era. From this time date the oldest fossils of animals with hard parts ever found. For many years, the main creatures were an odd group called **trilobites** (TRY-luh-bites). These sea crawlers were a bit like the lobsters of today. At their peak, almost 2500 kinds of trilobites swam the seas.

Fishes were the first creatures with a backbone. This was an important step forward. Animals would need backbones if they were ever to live on land. The Devonian Period, between 395 and 345 million years ago, is sometimes called the Age of Fishes. But don't think the early years would have made for good fishing. The first fish would have had a hard time biting on the hook. Like lampreys today, they had no jaws! Later fish did have jaws—and sharp teeth. One giant, named *Dinichthys* (Dine-IK-tis) was almost 11 metres (35 ft) long and was armed with dagger-like teeth.

Stepping Out

Something else was happening during the Age of Fishes, but it was taking place above the water's surface. Little by little, the plants of the sea had been starting to invade the land. They spread from the shallow waters into drier and drier areas. Over many years, the plants changed and grew more used to life on land. By the beginning of the next period of earth's history, the Carboniferous (Car-buh-NIF-er-us), the land was covered in lush forests.

It was also time for animal life to get on its feet. With a carpet of green to welcome them, some kinds of fish made their clumsy way on to dry land. These became the **amphibians** (am-FIB-ee-uns). They are a group of animals which spend part of their lives on land, but return to the water to have their young. The amphibians of the Carboniferous Period were not all as meek as today's frogs and newts. Some, such as 4.5-metre (15-ft) long *Eogyrinus* (EE-oh-gee-RYE-nus), looked more like a crocodile.

After millions of years, some of the amphibians had grown skin that would keep their insides moist even in very dry areas. The eggs that they laid now also had tough coverings. This meant they could be hatched out of water. These amphibians had become the first reptiles. The stage was set for the dinosaurs to make their appearance!

Day of the Dinosaur

The time when the dinosaurs lived is known as the **Mesozoic** (MEZ-uh-ZO-ik) **Era**—or earth's "middle years". The Mesozoic Era lasted for about 160 million years, between 225 and sixty-five million years ago. During this time, many different types of dinosaurs lived. The land and weather changed greatly during earth's Mesozoic Era. This created many different kinds of homes for many kinds of dinosaurs.

The Dinosaur Family Album

Picture a dinosaur. You probably imagine a creature the size of a building. It may have sharp, menacing teeth and long, curved claws. There were dinosaurs like this. But the terrifying meat-eaters like those we see in horror films made up just one group of the many kinds of dinosaurs. Almost all of the other groups were plant-eaters. Some of these plant-eaters were giants. But you'd have had little to fear from their teeth.

The main division in the dinosaur group was between those that had hips built like birds', and those that had hips like lizards'. It was on the lizard-hipped side of the dinosaur group that we find the fierce meat-eaters.

Lizard-hipped Dinosaurs

The earliest dinosaurs were members of a group called the **prosauropods** (pro-SORE-uh-pods). Compared to later dinosaurs, they were quite small. Most weighed only about 90-180 kilograms (200-300 lb).

All prosauropods were plant-eaters. They probably spent most of their time shuffling along on four legs, munching on low-growing plants. At times, they could rise up on their hind legs to reach taller branches.

The prosauropods led the way for the dinosaur group that includes the largest land animals of all time. These were the **sauropods** (SORE-uh-pods). Like their ancestors, the sauropods were four-legged plant-eaters that could stand upright if they wanted to. But some would not have needed to rise up on two legs to reach tree branches. Giant sauropods, such as *Apatosaurus* (Ah-PAT-uh-SORE-us) and *Diplodocus* (Dih-PLOD-uh-kus) would have reached high above many of today's treetops.

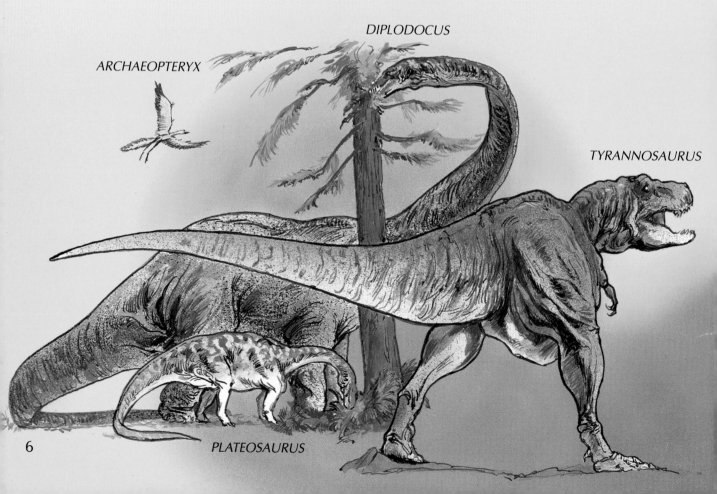

DIPLODOCUS

ARCHAEOPTERYX

TYRANNOSAURUS

PLATEOSAURUS

The mighty meat-eating dinosaurs were called **theropods** (THAIR-uh-pods). With huge jaws, sharp teeth and claws, and powerful hind legs, the theropods may have been among the most successful hunters ever. But some people think that even mighty *Tyrannosaurus* (Tie-RAN-uh-sore-es) might not have been so frightening after all. They may have been scavengers, animals that are more interested in dead than live meat.

Archaeopteryx (Ar-kee-OP-ter-ix) is another strange creature that might have been a member of the lizard-hipped group of dinosaurs. When the fossils of *Archaeopteryx* were found, they seemed to show a small, light-boned dinosaur. But the rock surrounding the bone fossils were covered in feather prints! Some people think *Archaeopteryx* might have been a link between dinosaurs and birds.

The Bird-hipped Dinosaurs

The bird-hipped group of dinosaurs included some very odd-looking creatures. Some of their strange designs might have been a way to protect themselves against meat-eaters.

Imagine a 10-metre (35-ft) long armadillo with a giant club on its tail. This was probably how a group of armoured dinosaurs called **ankylosaurs** (ang-KILE-uh-sores) must have looked. With the tough plates that covered their bodies, the ankylosaurs would have made a hard meal to chew on!

Their distant cousins, the **ceratopsians** (kair-uh-TOP-see-uns) and the **stegosaurs** (STEG-uh-sores) used armour to defend themselves too. The ceratopsians had a large bony frill protecting their necks. They also had long, spiky horns jutting out of their faces, like the horn of a rhinoceros. The line of bony triangles that ran down stegosaurs' backs might have been used for more than protection. These giant plates might have caught the sun's rays and warmed the stegosaurs' bodies.

A special group within the bird-hipped dinosaurs were like birds in another way. They are called the bird-footed dinosaurs, or **ornithopods** (or-NITH-uh-pods). One group of bird-footed dinosaurs, the *hadrosaurs* (HAD-ruh-sores), had jaws that looked like ducks' beaks. They also had head crests or long tubes reaching back over their shoulders. Scientists aren't sure what these were used for. They might have been a way for the animals to recognize each other or for them to make different noises.

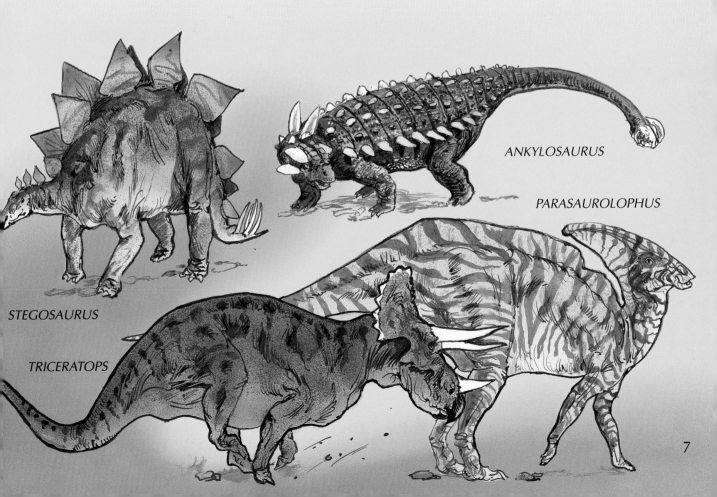

STEGOSAURUS

TRICERATOPS

ANKYLOSAURUS

PARASAUROLOPHUS

Sudden Ending

Something very mysterious happened sixty-five million years ago. We may never know what it was, but some secret killer struck the dinosaurs. Within a short time, these great creatures that had ruled the world for 160 million years disappeared from the face of the earth. What could have happened?

Scientists have many different ideas. The earth was cooling during the years when the dinosaurs disappeared. The animals that died might not have been able to survive a new, cooler **climate**. Another theory is that deadly diseases might have hit the dinosaurs as they travelled to new parts of the world. The earth's surface has changed a lot over its history. At certain times, land bridges appeared, allowing animals to move into new areas. Still another theory is that the end of the dinosaurs might have come from a giant meteor crash.

We may never know for certain what kind of deadly killer hit the dinosaurs. There may be many different reasons why their rule on earth ended.

They Weren't Alone!

The dinosaurs' mystery killer took many other victims. In fact, almost all large animals on land or in the seas were wiped out along with the dinosaurs. In all, scientists think that almost three-quarters of all animals disappeared at that time.

In the skies, the winged reptiles called **pterosaurs** (TAIR-uh-sores) disappeared. A whole range of ocean dwellers, including the long-necked **plesiosaurs** (PLEH-see-uh-sores), died out as well. Another group of victims were the **ammonites** (AM-uh-nites). These coil-shelled sea creatures had survived for about 220 million years. But they met their death together with the dinosaurs.

Survivors

Slowly, life on earth returned to normal. Plants grew and bloomed, and insects fed on them. Birds flew overhead. They nested in the branches of the young trees and ate what seeds and insects they could find. The new forests buzzed with life. Snakes, lizards, turtles, and small **mammals** made their homes there and competed with each other for food. Their biggest competitors, the dinosaurs, were gone. It was the beginning of a new age.

Many kinds of animals living today were alive during the time of the dinosaurs. Some of them were very successful even then and have changed little since. Other types of animals did not develop fully while the dinosaurs lived. But, with the dinosaurs gone, they came out of hiding and diversified into thousands of forms.

We don't know why some creatures were not affected by the great disaster that killed so many animals long ago. Perhaps these surviving animals were able to sleep through the period of danger the way some animals today sleep through winter. Perhaps they were able to live off seeds, berries, and roots that would still have been there to eat even if the plants died.

For whatever reason, many types of birds, insects, fish, mammals, amphibians, and reptiles survived. In the sixty-five million years since the dinosaurs disappeared, these survivors have branched out into huge groups of their own.

REPTILES

ISH

BIRDS

SOME MEMBERS OF THE KINGDOM ANIMALIA

NSECTS

MAMMALS

AMPHIBIANS

JELLYFISH

SHELLFISH

Birds

As the giant plesiosaurs swam the oceans millions of years ago, birds very much like today's gulls and herons flew overhead. There might have been as many as a thousand types of birds during the last years of the dinosaurs. Some scientists think that birds might actually have descended from the dinosaurs. If so, they are probably the dinosaurs' only living relatives.

We usually think of birds as rather small animals. The ostrich is the largest one that we know of today. But earlier birds included some of the world's giants!

Feathered Menace

Going back just over fifty million years, we find the wingless meat-eater *Diatryma* (Die-ah-TREE-mah) was living soon after the end of the dinosaurs. While *Diatryma* was not as large as meat-eating dinosaurs like *Tyrannosaurus*, it was probably the terror of its time! It lived before the mammals had become the powerful hunters they would later be. *Diatryma* was about the size and speed of an ostrich. But, with a huge head and hooked beak, it must have seemed like a monster to the lizards and small mammals it ate!

First Flyer?

The fossil bones of a crow-sized creature named *Protoavis* (Pro-toe-AV-iss) are shown here. *Protoavis* lived about 225 million years ago. Some scientists think it might have been an ancestor of modern birds. What do you notice about the size of *Protoavis*'s bones? Why do you think scientists might have problems finding ancient bird fossils?

The Hunt

The Maoris circled around the frightened group of moas. The giant birds had been surprised while feeding on the grassland. They looked around for escape. Against other animals, speed had always been their best defence. The moas' long, muscular legs could usually carry them to safety. But the giant birds had lost many battles against these people. How could creatures on just two weak legs defeat them when much swifter hunters could not? The moas' legs were faster than all others, but they could not outrun a flying spear or arrow from a human.

The Maoris closed in from all sides, showering the moas with their wooden missiles. A few of the giant birds staggered and fell. The people rushed in with clubs and knives to put an end to the fallen ones. Many Maori families could be fed by a single moa.

Elephant Birds

It would have taken a lot of worms to feed *Aepyornis* (EE-pee-OR-niss). This giant was one of an ancient group of birds known as the elephant birds. *Aepyornis* was about 3 metres (10 ft) high and might have weighed as much as 450 kilograms (1000 lb). But don't think you could have hitched a ride through the air on this bird's back. *Aepyornis* was far too heavy to get off the ground!

Fossils show that the elephant birds date back about two million years. They disappeared only a few hundred years ago. With all that meat on their bones, the elephant birds were probably hunted out of existence by people.

Another group of giant birds appeared about the same time as the elephant birds—but in a different part of the world. The wingless moas (MO-uhs) of New Zealand grew up to 2 metres (6 ft) high. None is left alive today. Like their elephant bird cousins, the moas were probably victims of human hunters—the Maori (Mah-ORE-ee) people of New Zealand.

Earliest Mammals

About 200 million years ago, a tiny animal similar to a mouse ran between and around the legs of the large reptiles that ruled the earth. This little creature was *Morganucodon* (Mor-gan-UH-ko-don), an insect-eater which was one of the first true mammals.

How did scientists decide that *Morganucodon* was different from other animal fossils dating back to the same time? One of the biggest differences was the kind of teeth this creature had. Reptiles have only one kind of teeth in their mouths. They may have thousands of teeth, but all are designed in the same way. *Morganucodon* had different kinds of teeth. Each kind was designed for a different task. This is one of the ways in which mammals differ from other animals.

Time Line of the Mammal

C E N O Z O I C	Quaternary PRESENT now to 40 000 years ago	
	40 000 years PLEISTOCENE to 2 million years ago	
	Tertiary PLIOCENE 2 to 7 million years ago	
	MIOCENE 7 to 26 million years ago	
	OLIGOCENE 26 to 38 million years ago	
	EOCENE 38 to 54 million years ago	
	PALAEOCENE 54 to 65 million years ago	

SKULL

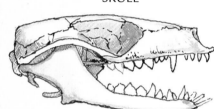

MORGANUCODON

ARMADILLO

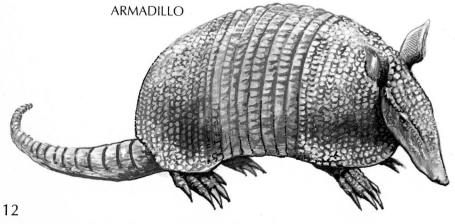

HEDGEHOG

What Makes a Mammal?

Mammals belong to the group of creatures that have backbones. There are actually three different groups of mammals live today, but most belong to the group called placental mammals. These give birth to living babies instead of laying eggs. After the babies are born, they are fed with milk from their mothers.

Mammals are the only animals that have a body covering of hair to keep them warm. Some, such as hedgehogs and armadillos, have changed their hair into different forms. These include spines and scales. Mammals have another trick that helps them survive in cool areas. They are all **warm-blooded**, or able to make their own body heat.

Except for some sea creatures, mammals all have four limbs. And like little *Morganucodon*, mammals have teeth that are designed to do different kinds of cutting and chewing.

- COVERING OF HAIR
- BACKBONE
- LIVE-BORN YOUNG FED WITH MOTHER'S MILK
- SPECIALIZED TEETH
- FOUR LIMBS
- WARM-BLOODED

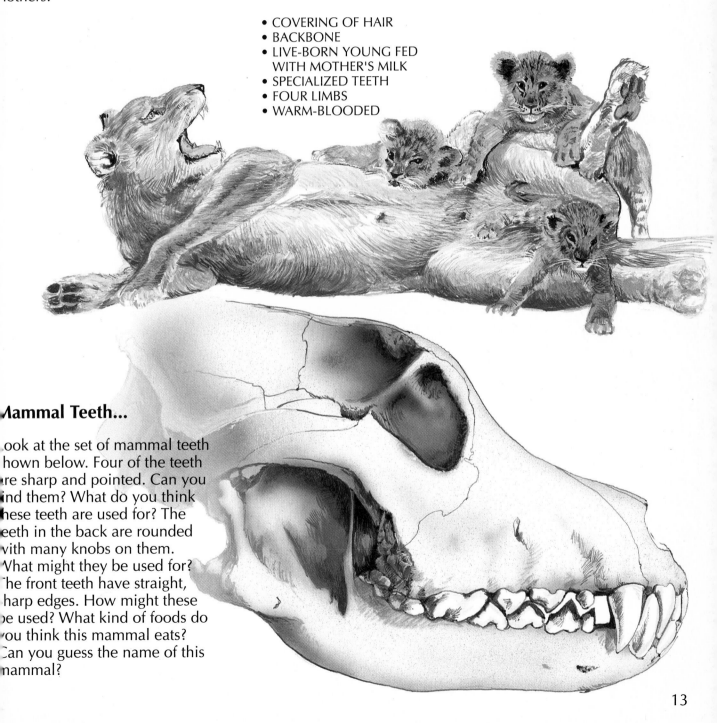

Mammal Teeth...

Look at the set of mammal teeth shown below. Four of the teeth are sharp and pointed. Can you find them? What do you think these teeth are used for? The teeth in the back are rounded with many knobs on them. What might they be used for? The front teeth have straight, sharp edges. How might these be used? What kind of foods do you think this mammal eats? Can you guess the name of this mammal?

New Lords of the Land

By the end of the dinosaur years, the main groups of mammals were alive and well. These included mammals that lived off plants, insects, and meat. But it was a little bit later, during the Eocene (EE-uh-SEEN) time of 54 to 38 million years ago, that mammals really started to come into their own. They developed many shapes and sizes to take advantage of different surroundings, and different types of diet. Since then, mammals have become the group of animals best suited to earth's many kinds of homes.

Meat-eating Mammals

Mammals that ate meat didn't start out as ferocious giants. Most early meat-eating mammals were somewhere in size between a badger and a sheep. Today, all meat-eaters belong to a group called Carnivora (car-NIV-uh-ra), which means "flesh-eater". But until about forty million years ago, the most successful meat-eaters belonged to a group called the **creodonts** (KREE-uh-donts). This name means "flesh tooth".

The creodonts were not very advanced. They had small brains, and their teeth and wrist bones were different from the **carnivores.** But in some ways, members of the creodont family were quite like certain meat-eaters today.

Oxyaena (OX-eye-EE-nah), with its short legs and powerful body, probably looked a good deal like a wolverine. *Tritemnodon* (Try-TEM-noh-don) was another creodont. With its slim body and long legs, it was a fast runner for its time. It probably looked something like a hyena. But none of these animals was a relative of living meat-eaters. Most of the creodonts disappeared at the end of the Eocene time, although a few hung on until just a few million years ago.

The creodonts may have been "outsmarted" by their cousins, the carnivores. With their large brains, the carnivores would have been better at hunting the plant-eaters. As the years went by, the plant-eaters were becoming faster and cleverer.

The two main groups of carnivores are the cats and their relatives, and the dogs and their relatives. These two groups have different hunting styles and different body parts to go with them.

OXYAENA (CREODONT)

TRITEMNODON (CREODONT)

PSEUDOCYNODICTIS (CREODONT)

CARNIVORES
CAT FAMILY

LION

GENET

HYENA

CIVET

DOG FAMILY

DOG

BADGER

WEASEL

BEAR

RACCOON

Wild Cats!

The fluffy kittens we love to tease with balls of string had some tough relatives millions of years ago! The cats developed as one of the greatest groups of hunters. With their sleek, muscular bodies, as well as their sharp teeth and claws, these meat-eaters were feared by animals often much bigger than them.

Until about two million years ago, most cats were **sabre-toothed.** They were a powerful group. Their upper fangs were long and pointed like sabres (swords with slightly curved blades). Modern cats have fangs that are about the same length for the upper and lower set. The sabre-toothed cats used their long upper teeth to hunt in a different style from modern cats. They had to. Many of the animals they hunted were larger and had thicker hides than the animals which today's cats eat.

Modern cats feed on swift, medium-sized runners like deer, antelope, and horses. The cats attack by leaping on to their victims' backs and using their powerful jaws to break the neck. This kills the animal quickly before it can escape. But the sabre-toothed cats lived in the days of huge plant-eaters such as rhinoceroses and mastodons. (Mastodons were large ancient relatives of the elephants.) These creatures were slow-moving, but were protected by their size and thic hides. Instead of killing quickly the sabre-toothed cats probably used their long fangs to slash at the victim's hide. Although the animal could continue to move it would slowly bleed to death.

The great sabre-toothed cats gave way to modern cats as the numbers of fast-running plant-eaters increased. Sabre-toothed cats died out when their main food, the mastodons, disappeared 8000 years ago.

Bear-dogs

In the grasslands during Miocene (MY-uh-SEEN) times, between twenty-six and seven million years ago, a squat hunter chases its prey, an early horse. Although *Daphoenodon* (Daf-FEE-noh-on) is not large, it is a good hunter, with its thick, strong body. The horse soon weakens from *Daphoenodon's* bites and slashes. It falls to the ground and is leapt upon by the hunter.

Daphoenodon belonged to a group known as the bear-dogs. It was probably an early ancestor of the modern bear. Dogs developed as a group well suited to plains hunting. Fast runners with long snouts and blunt claws, these dogs worked well in packs to wear down their victims. Millions of years ago, the bears branched off from this line of dogs. The bears grew to greater and greater sizes over the years.

Cave Bear

The most powerful bear ever was the great cave bear. It lived during Pleistocene (PLY-stuh-SEEN) times between two million and 40 000 years ago. This mighty creature was about twice the size of a grizzly bear. The cave bear may have weighed about 400 kilograms (800 lb). With a thick coat of fur, the cave bear was well protected for the ice ages of the Pleistocene times.

While other creatures died out from the cold during this time, the cave bears were probably killed off by an even greater hunter. Their teeth, claws, and skulls have been found in caves where humans of the time lived. It is probable that cave bears were hunted and killed in great numbers and taken back to the caves to be eaten.

Plant-eating Mammals

In the early morning, *Phenacodus* (Fen-nah-KO-dus) shuffles through the undergrowth of the forest. It stops and chews on bushes, picking and choosing to find the newest and softest leaves. *Phenacodus* keeps a careful eye out as it eats. Although it is a fairly large plant-eater for the time it lived in, it must beware of hungry meat-eaters.

Phenacodus was one of the earliest ancestors of modern plant-eating mammals. About the size of a sheep, it had a rather thick body, a long tail, and rounded cheek teeth that were good for chewing on soft plants. *Phenacodus*'s feet had five hoofed toes.

The group of mammals that *Phenacodus* belonged to was called the **condylarths** (KHON-dee-larths). Over millions of years, this group would lead to an amazing variety of animals. Each was specially adapted for a certain kind of diet and way of life. From the condylarths come all of the main types of plant-eating mammals we know today. These include horses, elephants, rhinoceroses, deer, pigs, and hippopotamuses.

Life on the Run

As the earth became drier, one group of animals took to the open life of the plains. Over millions of years, these creatures grew to become swift runners. Their teeth became well designed for a diet of tough prairie grasses. With their long, slender legs, powerful muscles, and hoofed feet, horses are the long-distance runners of the animal world.

Scientists have quite a clear picture of the horses' family tree. The fossil record stretches back about fifty million years to a small forest dweller called *Hyracotherium* (Hi-RACK-uh-THEER-ee-um), or *Eohippus* (E uh-HIP-pus). This last name means "dawn horse". *Hyracotherium* was about the size of a modern fox and had four toes on its front feet and three toes on its hind feet. But already the beginnings of the horse line can be seen in *Hyracotherium*. Later, *Mesohippus* (Mez-uh-HIP-pus) *Merychippus* (Mare-rick-HIP-pus), and *Equus* (EK-wis) woul follow in the horse line.

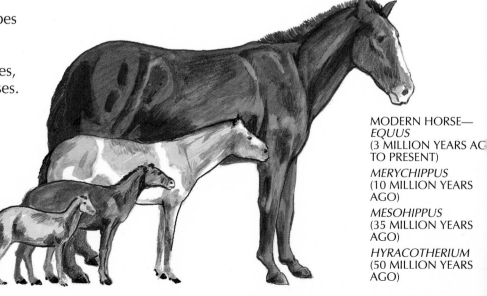

MODERN HORSE—
EQUUS
(3 MILLION YEARS AC
TO PRESENT)

MERYCHIPPUS
(10 MILLION YEARS
AGO)

MESOHIPPUS
(35 MILLION YEARS
AGO)

HYRACOTHERIUM
(50 MILLION YEARS
AGO)

The Bulky Cousins

The horses have an unlikely set of distant cousins. These cousins are also plains dwellers, but developed size instead of speed to defend themselves against hunters. Today's rhinoceros shares *Hyracotherium* as an ancestor with the horse. An early group of rhinoceroses was long limbed and horse-like. These were the Hyracodons (Hi-RACK-oh-dons) who lived in Oligocene (OLLEE-go-SEEN) times, between 38 and 26 million years ago.

But the main line of the rhinoceros family developed more bulk and a thick skin for protection. Today's rhinoceroses are very small compared to some of their ancient relatives. *Paraceratherium* (Par-ah-kair-uh-THEER-ee-um) was the largest mammal that ever walked on land. It stood 5.5 metres (18 ft) high at the shoulders and probably weighed about 18 tonnes. Because of its gigantic size, *Paraceratherium* could easily browse among the leaves of tall trees. It must have stripped many forests to feed its huge body.

Paraceratherium did not develop horns the way its cousin *Brontotherium* (Bron-toe-THEER-ee-um) did. This creature had a strange double set of curved horns on its nose. No one really knows why *Brontotherium* developed such huge, blunt horns. The name of this 5-tonne animal means "thunder beast".

A WHITE RHINOCEROS OF TODAY COULD HAVE PASSED UNDERNEATH THE BELLY OF PARACERATHERIUM

PARACERATHERIUM

BRONTOTHERIUM

Focus on Feet

One of the most important things that changed with time was the horse family's feet. Over millions of years, the toes slowly evolved into hooves. *Hyracotherium* had four toes in front and three at the back. *Mesohippus* had three toes on each foot. *Merychippus* also had three toes on each foot, but walked only on the middle toes. The foot of a modern horse, or *Equus*, has only one "toe"—its hoof. In what ways do you think a single hoof is better for running on than many toes?

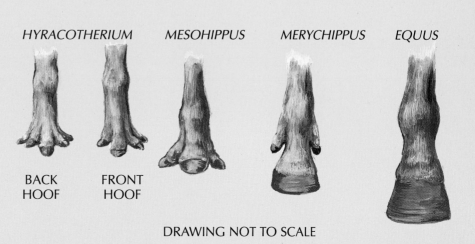

HYRACOTHERIUM   *MESOHIPPUS*   *MERYCHIPPUS*   *EQUUS*

BACK HOOF   FRONT HOOF

DRAWING NOT TO SCALE

Ancient Elephants

With a downward twist of his head, *Deinotherium* (Dine-noh-THEER-ee-um) snaps off the branch that is nestled beneath his downward-curving tusks. Now that the branch is broken free, the giant uses his short trunk to grasp and pull it into his mouth. He chews slowly, grinding up the soft wood and leaves.

Deinotherium looked quite similar to modern elephants, although he seemed to have his tusks pointed in the wrong direction. But *Deinotherium* was probably only a distant cousin of the animal line that led to today's elephants.

The real elephant ancestor probably looked like little

Moeritherium (Moh-ree-THEER-ee-um). This animal from Eocene times was about the size of a pig. It had small, tusk-like front teeth, but no trunk. Another creature living along-side *Moeritherium* looked more like a modern elephant. *Palaeomastodon* (Pay-lee-oh-MASS-tuh-don) had a short trunk and small upper and lower sets of tusks.

The elephants didn't develop along a single line. There are many branches on this family tree. Almost every combination of trunks and tusks has been tried at least once! *Platybelodon* (PLAH-tee-buh-LOWE-don), which appeared about twenty million years ago, was one of the strangest. It had only short upper tusks and a squared-off lower pair of tusks in its mouth. *Platybelodon* may have used its long, flat lower jaw like a shovel, to scoop plants out of the earth.

Mammals of the Sea

A strange set of cousins might have come from the same ancestor as the elephants. Sea cows are a group of mammals that took to the ocean many millions of years ago. They might be descended from whatever creature led the way to *Moeritherium* and *Palaeomastodon*. This common ancestor probably lived part of its life on land and part in the water.

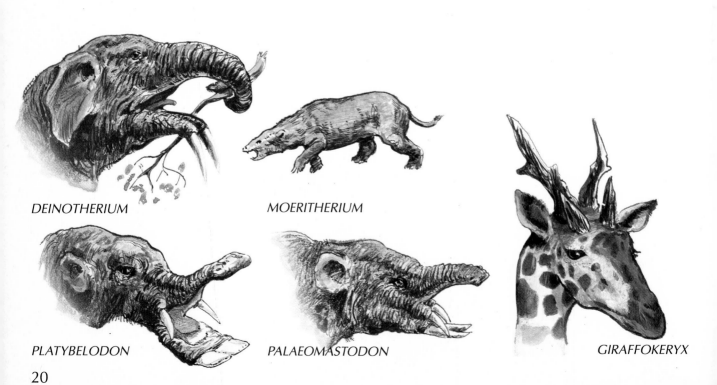

DEINOTHERIUM

MOERITHERIUM

PLATYBELODON

PALAEOMASTODON

GIRAFFOKERYX

Odd Bunch

The main group of plant-eating mammals alive today is a strange assortment. Pigs, cattle, deer, antelopes, camels, and hippopotamuses all belong to the same mammal family. They don't look like they have much in common. But they do—from the ankles down.

All of these animals share a special bone. It allows their ankles to move easily backwards or forwards, but very little from side to side. They also have an even number of toes on each foot so that their weight is carried between the middle toes.

Mud Happy

Pigs and hippopotamuses love to roll in the mud. But pigs are much better suited to dry land than their hippopotamus cousins. Modern hippopotamuses spend a great deal of their time in shallow waters. An earlier cousin, *Hippopotamus gorgops* of Pleistocene times, might have been even more at home in the water. Its eyes were high on its head in little bulges that would have allowed it to see, even when its body and most of its head were underwater.

Counting Toes

Look at the mammal feet pictured here. Can you tell which ones belong to the same group as pigs and deer? Count their toes to see. Can you guess which animals all these feet belong to?

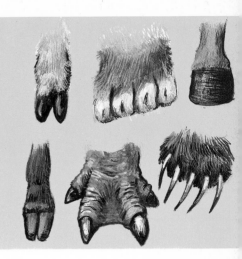

Horns and Antlers

Other members of this even-toed mammal group developed some dazzling head pieces. They might have been used to protect or call attention to the mammals themselves. Still, some of the showier pieces might have been too bulky to be very practical!

Not long before our time, parts of Ireland were roamed by a group of deer called *Megaloceros* (Meh-ga-loss-SAIR-us). It must have been difficult for these creatures to hold their heads up. They were crowned with the largest sets of antlers ever grown. Some spread as wide as 3 metres (10 ft) across.

In much earlier times, North Africa was home to distant cousins of the giraffe called *Prolibytherium* (PRO-lih-bee-THEER-ee-um). But you might not have recognized these giraffes. About the size of sheep, they had short legs and necks. On their heads, they had huge plate-like horns that spread across their skulls.

Another creature called *Giraffokeryx* (Gee-raf-foh-CARE-ix), looked a little more like modern giraffes. They were long necked and had long, slender legs. But these ancient Indian cousins of the modern giraffe had two sets of horns, one just above their eyes, and the other on the back of the head.

MEGALOCEROS

Down from the Trees

Twenty-six million years ago, the earth was becoming drier and drier. Lush forests that had once covered great areas of land were slowly changing to vast plains of grass. With fewer and fewer trees to live in, competition in the forest got tough!

Some tree dwellers came down out of the branches to try out life on the ground. *Ramapithecus* (Rah-mah-PITH-eh-kus) was one of the earliest ape-like creatures. Like its swinging cousins, the monkeys, *Ramapithecus* had long arms. And it had toes that could grip as well as its fingers. But it probably spent much of its time down on the ground. There, *Ramapithecus* would shuffle along on its hind legs and front knuckles, searching for food.

Out for a Stroll

Two hunched creatures make their way carefully across the plain. On two legs, they move a little awkwardly. But they are able to see for great distances over the grassland. They can spot both danger and food from a long way off.

A gentle rain had fallen during the night. The ground is soft under foot. As the pair make their way along, they leave behind a trail of footprints. Millions of years later, people will wonder what kind of creature might have left these tracks behind.

These footprints were found in Laetoli, Tanzania, in Africa.

They showed that there were ape-like animals walking upright on two legs almost four million years ago. The tracks are not the only clues we have to these creatures. Many fossil bones of the group called *Australopithecus* (Awe-STRAIL-low-PITH-eh-kus) have been found in southern and eastern Africa. *Australopithecus* means "southern ape".

The fossils show that the *Australopithecus* group was like humans in some ways. Their thigh bones were quite like ours, so that they were probably able to walk with their legs directly under their hips. The backbones of the "southern apes" also supported their skulls from underneath. The backbones of modern apes are attached to the backs of their skulls. This gives them their hunched appearance. Apes also have legs that bend outwards from the hips. They can only walk short distances on two legs.

The *Australopithecus* group was quite different from us in many ways. Their pelvic bones were more like an ape's than a human's. They were much smaller in overall size, and they had brains only about half as large as ours. But scientists put them in the group of human-like animals called **hominids** (HOM-ih-nids).

What Makes a Human?

If someone asked you what made people special, you might say: "people can think" and "people have feelings". Or you might say: "people make things" and "people communicate with each other". Scientists have a hard time agreeing about which of these things are unique to human beings and which aren't. This makes it doubly hard to decide when the first humans appeared. Several types of ape-like creatures began to look and behave more like human beings in the past few millions of years. Scientists look mainly at the size and shape of the skull to separate true humans from the early hominids.

Toolmaker

Almost two million years ago, an ape-like creature sat on an outcrop of rock. In her hands, she held two pieces of stone. Clumsily, she banged one stone downwards on the edge of the other. A small piece of rock flew off. She banged again at the stone. Another chip of rock broke away. Over and over, she chipped away at the stone until finally it showed an uneven but sharp edge.

The toolmaker picked up a nearby piece of bone left over from an earlier hunt. She placed it on the ground beneath her and brought her crude blade down upon it with all her strength. The wedge cut deeply into the bone and lodged there. Satisfied, she removed her tool and headed back to join the rest of her group.

The toolmaker belonged to a group called **Homo habilis** ("handy man") that appeared almost two million years ago in Africa. The crude tools made by *Homo habilis* are called "Oldowan" (OHL-dew-on) after the Olduvai Gorge in Tanzania. This is where "handy man" fossils were first discovered.

Traveller

The early hominids all seem to have lived in Africa. This is the only continent on which such early fossils of them have been found. Then, about 700 000 years ago, a group called **Homo erectus** ("upright man") headed north. Eventually, they spread through Europe and northern Asia.

Homo erectus had to learn a few new tricks to survive in the much colder climate of the north. These hominids might have been the first to have homes with "central heating". Fossils of Homo erectus have been found in a cave in northern China. In the cave were charcoal and ash from an ancient fire. We don't know if the Homo erectus group was able to start fires or if they had to "collect" it from the wild. They could "collect" fire from such natural events as lightning strikes or brush fires. No matter how they got fire, they certainly seemed to have used it to cook food and to keep warm.

Using Fire

Today, we have many devices for cooking and heating. Stoves, electric cookers, and furnaces are much safer than an open flame. But for thousands of years, fire was all we had! In what ways do you think early creatures like Homo erectus might have used fire? How do you think fire might have made them different from hominids that did not have it?

Master Hunter

The woolly rhinoceros lowers his head and snorts. His eyes see the two-legged hunter in front of him. But even as he prepares to charge, his body is racked with pain and fear. He is surrounded by his most dangerous enemy. Already, the rhinoceros's hide is punctured by a dozen spears. They jut out from his shaggy coat like porcupine quills.

Weakly, he stumbles towards the hunter. His great horns are aimed at the stomach of the Neanderthal (Nee-AN-dur-THOL). The charge is expected. The Neanderthal hunter neatly steps aside in time to sink a spear deeply into the rhinoceros's neck. Dizzy from loss of blood, the woolly giant falls to the ground. A shower of spears and rocks rains down upon him. A team of Neanderthal hunters moves in to finish off the dying animal.

These great hunters of the ice ages, the Neanderthals, were close cousins of ours. They were probably a little shorter than modern humans. But the Neanderthals had powerful bodies, and their brains were slightly larger than ours. Remains have been found which show that they lived in many parts of Europe, Asia, and North Africa. They survived well in the cold, living mostly in caves. They hunted ice-age giants such as woolly rhinoceroses, woolly mammoths, horses, deer, and the mighty cave bears.

Artist

The woman sits close to the light of the fire, squinting into her bowl. Not satisfied, she takes two soft, dark rocks and grinds more black powder into the bowl mixture. Now the colour is right, but the paste is too thick and dry. She stirs in another drop of the warm oil that has been skimmed from animal fat. The paint is ready now.

Behind her, her son is busy at the wall of the cave. Already he has completed the outline of a bison in brilliant red. With the black prepared by his mother, he will paint in hoofs and horns.

Remains of people very much like ourselves were found in south-west France in 1868. These people from 30 000 years ago were called Cro-Magnon, after the region where they were discovered. Besides being hunters with a wide range of tools and weapons, the Cro-Magnon were the first artists we know of. They carved pictures into objects made from wood, ivory, and bone. And they left behind many beautiful paintings of the animals they hunted. We don't really know why they made these paintings. They might have been for good luck during the hunt. Or these ancient cave dwellers might just have been expressing themselves as we do today by writing and painting.

Who Were the First Humans?

The name scientists have given to human beings is **Homo sapiens**. It means "wise man". Although the Neanderthals, were close enough to ourselves to be included in *Homo sapiens*, they were probably not our ancestors. Their family line ended about 40 000 years ago.

Homo sapiens fossils date back to about 250 000 years ago in Germany, France, and England. One tiny piece of jawbone found in Hungary may be from a *Homo sapiens* who lived 450 000 years ago. Fossils show that some *Homo erectus* lived up to about 40 000 years ago. So *Homo sapiens* and *Homo erectus* overlapped in time. Many scientists think that *Homo sapiens* developed in Africa and then spread to other parts of the world. In some areas, *Homo erectus* might have lived alongside modern humans for hundreds of thousands of years before disappearing.

27

Brain Power in Action

Human beings have come to dominate the world in ways the dinosaurs never dreamed of. Unlike other creatures, humans are not limited to areas where the climate and surroundings are comfortable. We can mould our world to suit us!

The greatest advantage we have over other animals is our human brain. With this brain, we do not have to be strong, or have thick coats of fur for the winter, or fast legs for escaping danger. We have the brain power to invent tools. These do many of the tasks that other animals' bodies must do for them.

Language—Speaking and Writing

Our greatest tool may be our language. Other animals can communicate with one another. Bees have complex dances that tell other members of the hive where honey can be found. Dolphins and whales may be able to send messages for great distances through the oceans. But none of these animals can record their messages so that years later other members of their group can learn from them.

The earliest record we have of written language dates back over 5000 years. A group of people called the Sumerians (Soo-MAIR-ee-uns) used picture symbols to tell stories. Since then, many different systems of writing have come into use. Writing has allowed groups of people to learn from each othe and to pass on knowledge to their children. This sharing of knowledge among human beings has led to great inventions and discoveries. These, in turn, have led to better, longer lives for many people.

28

Numbers—the Language of Mathematics

Numbers might be the most common language used in the world. Even where people speak in different languages, the same system of counting and calculation is used by scientists. The earliest use of mathematics we have found comes from the people of ancient Babylon. About 4000 years ago, they were cutting wedge shapes in clay tablets. This is how they kept track of what they owned, lost, or gave away.

Building our World

Most animals are suited to one type of climate. Humans have developed ways to live in the heat of the tropics or in the cold of the polar regions. Proper shelter and clothing have helped people adjust to these harsh surroundings.

From the time that the first human took shelter in a cave, people have built better and better homes. The earliest built homes were probably just temporary shelters made from branches and mud. Later, humans learned to build with wood and stone. Heating was once provided only by fire. In some parts of the world now, homes are heated by gas, electricity, and even the collected power of the sun. Depending on what materials are around them, humans can build a shelter from almost anything!

Going Places

Compared with the galloping legs of a horse, the two legs of human beings are not a very fast way to travel. But humans have spread to every continent on earth—and visited the moon too! We are the greatest travellers in earth's history because of the things we have built to take us to different places.

We have come a long way since the first wheel was placed under a heavy load to make moving it easier. Many people in the world still use animals to pull heavy loads. But many other people now rely on machine engines thousands of times stronger than a horse or an ox. Today, humans can travel over land by bicycle, car, train, or bus. To cross water, we have canoes, sailing ships, speedboats, and huge ocean liners. If these take too long, we can always fly in jets and planes.

What Will Tomorrow Bring?

It has been only between 300 000 and 450 000 years since the first human appeared. That may seem like a long time. But in the great length of earth's history, it's no more than the blink of an eye!

In this very short span of time, we humans have changed the face of the earth. Many of these changes have led to good. Cures have been found for a number of diseases, and almost every new invention makes life easier. But some of these changes have not led to good. The poor use and at times abuse of the earth's resources have resulted in polluted water, air, and land.

The earth is the shared responsibility of every living thing on it. We all must do our part to preserve its beauty and conserve its resources—thick, green forests; crystal-clear lakes; fresh, clean air. Hopefully, the highly developed brains we have will find new and better ways of doing just that.

Perhaps studying the dinosaurs can teach us how. After all, these amazing creatures survived for over 160 million years. For animals once thought of as "stupid", they were very successful! Let's hope we can do as well as they did—and better.